SPEN VALLEY

CLECKHEATON, HECKMONDWIKE, LIVERSEDGE AND GOMERSAL

Patricia Yvonne

Annabel

1+

Spen Valley on a map published in 1947. Heckmondwike, unlike Cleckheaton and Liversedge, was not included in Spenborough Urban District.

IMAGES
of England

SPEN VALLEY

CLECKHEATON, HECKMONDWIKE, LIVERSEDGE AND GOMERSAL

Compiled by
Norman Ellis

TEMPUS

First published 2001
Copyright © Norman Ellis, 2001

Tempus Publishing Limited
The Mill, Brimscombe Port,
Stroud, Gloucestershire, GL5 2QG

ISBN 0 7524 2172 7

Typesetting and origination by
Tempus Publishing Limited
Printed in Great Britain by
Midway Clark Printing, Wiltshire

Royal visit of King George V and Queen Mary to Cleckheaton, 10 July 1912. The entourage is ascending Westgate. 'We had a good day here on Wednesday. The King and Queen looked well. Hope you are having a good time and that your mother is a little better.' So wrote H.M. Craven when he sent the postcard from Cleckheaton to Miss Pearson in Bournemouth on 13 July 1912.

Contents

Acknowledgements

The author appreciates the valuable help given by many people in the preparation of this book. Thanks to the staff at Cleckheaton Library and Dewsbury Museum (Kirklees Metropolitan Council). Thanks to Robert Oates of Mirfield for the loan of fourteen postcards. Useful information was gleaned from back issues of the *Cleckheaton Advertiser & Spen Valley Times*. Finally, thanks to those who produced the original postcards.

Introduction

The Spen Valley is a unclearly defined district in the industrial part of West Yorkshire. It sits unashamedly within a triangle formed by Bradford, Huddersfield and Wakefield. Since time immemorial, the River Spen has twisted and turned through the region. Its waters have occasionally breached their banks, as if to affirm its presence. Good humouredly, some of the local people call the district Cleckheckmondsedge. This is a compound of the names of the area's three towns – Cleckheaton, Heckmondwike and Liversedge. The sobriquet has not been widely adopted. It takes no account of Gomersal, which can claim to have more history than the other three together. The book is about Cleckheaton, Heckmondwike, Liversedge, Gomersal and a sprinkling of other places, all of which, by one criterion or another, can be regarded as constituents of the Spen Valley. Cleckheaton, Liversedge and Gomersal were, in 1915, amalgamated to form Spenborough Urban District. This was further enlarged in 1937 to take in Birkenshaw, Hartshead and Hunsworth. This medley became a municipal borough in 1955. Heckmondwike remained detached until 1974 when, along with Spenborough, it became part of Kirklees Metropolitan Borough.

The Spen Valley may have existed for a long time, but the name was only formally adopted towards the end of the nineteenth century. Various parts of the valley were mentioned in *Domesday Book*, but the population was then light and well scattered. The valley of the River Spen and its environs must have looked sublime. In medieval times, the families were largely self-supporting, growing their own crops, keeping a few sheep and processing wool for their clothes. Amid the idyllic surroundings, life was not easy. Different families often worked together in the fields. For the land they cultivated, households paid rent to the lord of the manor and sometimes provided labour for the lord's own fields.

The sheep rearing and self-sufficient production of wool through all its various processes inevitably led to a small profit-motivated cottage industry. The work was often done in the upper storeys of stone cottages. A number of trustees organized the building of the large Gomersal Cloth Hall in 1775. This brick building, with two projecting wings, stood on the site of the later Thomas Burnley's mill. Twice weekly, on Mondays and Thursdays, at the George and Dragon Inn (later the George) on Heckmondwike's Westgate, merchants came to buy finished blankets from the cloth-makers. When trade expanded, the landlord arranged the erection of Heckmondwike's first blanket hall behind the George and Dragon. A bell on top of the two-storey building, which opened in 1811, was rung to signal commencement of business. One hour later, when the bell was rung to announce closure, clients retired to the adjacent pub for liquid refreshment. In 1839, continued expansion led to the building of a larger Heckmondwike Blanket Hall. It had seventeen rooms which were each available for rental to local blanket weavers for around £3 per year. Emergence of the Spen Valley as a textile region was reinforced by the appearance of shrewd entrepreneurs, many of them already wealthy, who became mill-owners on a relatively big scale. The stone-built mills, with their tall chimneys, blended reasonably well into their surroundings, as did many of the rows of workers' houses. But much of the landscape changed dramatically. A degree of speciality evolved. Cleckheaton became known for manufacture of card clothing: strips of leather into which numerous small iron staples were set. The strips were fixed to the rollers of machines which were used for carding wool prior to spinning and weaving. Heckmondwike became famous for carpet weaving. The Liversedge area had less specialization than its neighbours.

The industrial boom was fraught with problems. The livelihood of croppers (cloth finishers) in Liversedge was threatened in 1812, due to a recession caused by the Napoleonic War. The croppers joined the Luddite movement. They ambushed a wagon-load of machinery bound for William Cartwright's mill at Rawfolds and later attacked the mill itself. The rallying cry of the Chartist movement (formed in 1838), which agitated for democratic ideals that are now taken for granted, was heeded by many working-class people. The Chartists' call for strike action led to thousands of their supporters marching on Cleckheaton's St Peg Mill in 1842, in an attempt to remove sealing plugs from boilers. These 'Plug Riots' were thwarted by the presence of the Yorkshire Hussars and a contingent of special constables.

Two railway companies served the Spen Valley. The Lancashire & Yorkshire Railway arrived in 1848; the London & North Western Railway in 1900. The hilly terrain meant that the lines were heavily engineered, with stations sometimes inconveniently sited. The towns and townships of the Spen Valley reached a heyday in the first decade of the twentieth century. This coincided with the heyday of the picture postcard. Intended mainly as a means of communication, postcards, particularly photographic ones, also provide a valuable social commentary. Without them, this pictorial book would not have been possible. When, later in the twentieth century, economic depression struck, the area fared better than many others because, despite some specialization in manufacturing, there was also a degree of diversity. The growth of industry generated a lot of wealth, but not for everyone. At the peak of Spen Valley's prosperity, most people earned barely enough to support their families, with little surplus for holidays, times of illness or saving for old age. Menfolk found some solace in the working men's clubs. But it was the Nonconformist places of worship, mainly Congregational and Methodist, which provided a whole range of activities for men, women and children. The attractive chapels, some of the finest in Yorkshire, contrasted sharply with the daunting mills. In the latter half of the twentieth century, the mill and chapel buildings became a liability for differing reasons.

What's in a name? How did the individual, and often strange, Spen Valley names originate? Their derivation sometimes smacks more of conjecture than certainty. Cleckheaton is probably derived from Old English, meaning 'a high farmstead', and indicates that the first settlers were Anglo-Saxons. Some later poll tax returns showed it as 'Heton Clak', which likely means a village on open moorland. In the fourteenth century, some strips of land designated for farming were called Upper and Lower Whitecliffe, Peaselands and Tofts. Today, these occur as local street names. A Spen Valley map published just before the Industrial Revolution does not include Cleckheaton (or any similar name) but shows White Chapel. The actual chapel originated in the twelfth century. Liversedge may originate from the Old English *ilif* for 'a flood or pool' and *secg*, or 'rough grass or sedge'. Heckmondwike may derive from *Aegmond* (a chief's name) and *wic*, or 'home, farm or village'. Gomersal possibly comes from *guma* ('a man') and *alh* or *sel* ('a hall, meeting place' or 'piece of land').

Liversedge was once described as the keystone of the valley because, when Domesday Book was compiled, it was the only area with a significant population, other parts having been devastated by William the Conqueror after the Norman invasion. In 1893, the *Bradford Argus* claimed that there was no such place as Liversedge, but only High Town, Little Town, Robert Town and some other towns. Three hundred years ago, they were known as Great Liversedge, Little Liversedge and Liversedge Robert. Then the Liversedge element was dropped. The industrial heartland of Liversedge, situated near the river, appropriately became known as Millbridge.

When a short item was being recorded about Cleckheaton by BBC Radio, the producer, probably from down south, decided he did not like the name. 'Change it to Bradford or Leeds', he said. The audacity of the man!

Spen Valley mills may have closed and factories changed hands. Several notable buildings have been demolished. Urban expansion, much of it consisting of new housing, is very evident. But the Spen Valley which we see today is still largely a product of the Industrial Revolution.

Norman Ellis
January 2001

One
Cleckheaton

Albion Street, Cleckheaton, looking towards Bradford Road and the Town Hall, *c*. 1905. At the extreme right is part of the premises of John Siddal, printer. He founded the firm in 1845.

Bradford Road and Cleckheaton Town Hall, 1905. Built partly with money raised by public subscription, the Town Hall was opened in 1892. Apart from office accommodation for various managers, inspectors and clerks, the building housed a large public hall which was much used for concerts, dances and political meetings.

Bradford Road, Cleckheaton. This photograph is similar to the top one, but was taken almost three decades later. A new Yorkshire Penny Bank building is visible on the site of the former Freeman, Hardy & Willis footwear shop near the Town Hall.

Bradford Road, Cleckheaton, *c.* 1905. Church Street is behind the end of the tramcar. To the right of the Freeman, Hardy & Willis establishment is the Spot Cash Tailoring shop.

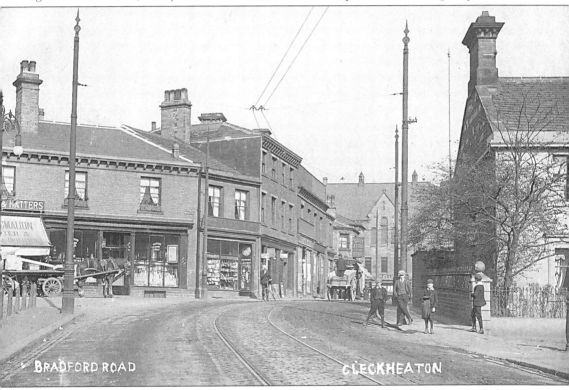

Bradford Road, Cleckheaton, *c.* 1905, with the lower end of Market Street on the left. At No. 1 Market Street (the building with two upstairs windows) is the shop of Kelita Marsden, watchmaker and jeweller. In the far distance is the Conservative Club, built in 1887.

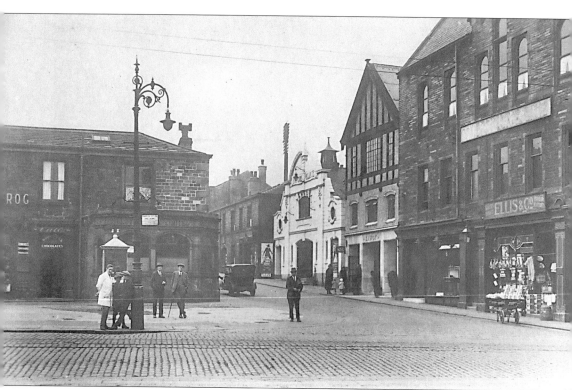

Albion Street from Bradford Road, *c.* 1928. Several interesting buildings enhance this view. Behind the telephone box stands the Lloyds Bank building. On the right is part of the Conservative Club. Its ground floor had been designed to incorporate retail outlets. Visible here are the shops of Ellis & Co., provision merchants, and the Public Benefit Boot Co. (nearly off the picture, far right) which, like Freeman, Hardy & Willis Ltd, opened shops in many northern towns. Further up the hill, the light-coloured building is the Picture Palace, which was opened in 1911 by local entrepreneur Walter Goodall. Films were previously shown in the Town Hall. Below the Picture Palace is another cinema, the Savoy, with some half-timbering. It opened in 1923 and also formed part of the Goodall empire. The Picture Palace closed after a fire in 1960. The Savoy, having temporarily switched to bingo, finally stopped showing films in 1972.

Bradford Road and the corner of Albion Street, Cleckheaton, *c.* 1950. In the centre of the picture, beyond the Conservative Club, is the main entrance to the Savoy Cinema, which seated approximately 1,200 people. Signs of the times are the Belisha Beacon and increase in motorized traffic.

Bradford Road, Cleckheaton, showing the stretch of road in the previous view, but looking in the opposite direction, 1950. The Town Hall and Savoy Cinema are visible.

Cleckheaton, *c.* 1948. This panorama of the town centre was photographed from near Cleckheaton LNWR Station, looking to the west. The viaduct gave access across the River Spen to the station and goods yard. Identifiable in the distance are Central Methodist Chapel, St John's Parish Church and the Town Hall.

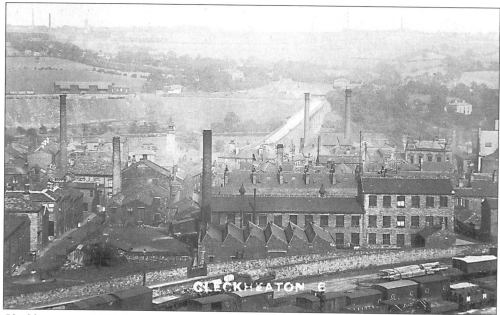

Cleckheaton, *c.* 1905. This vista was taken from the Prospect area, looking in the opposite direction to the top view. The viaduct is in the centre. Cleckheaton LNWR goods warehouse, signal box and station are half way up the hillside. In the foreground is part of Cleckheaton L&YR goods yard with, nearby, a congested area of factories and homes.

Whitechapel Road, Cleckheaton, looking south, *c.* 1908. Many of the dwellings shown, including back-to-back houses, have now gone. Some of them accommodated workers at Chairbarrows Colliery, the remains of which, including the spoil heap, are visible on the right. The pit was active in the latter half of the nineteenth century.

Wappy Nicket, Cleckheaton, 1906. An elderly gentleman pauses on the footpath leading from Prospect Road to Peaseland Road, and passing Gladstone House and Carlton House. The origin of the name is uncertain, but may be a derivation of snicket, a passageway or short cut.

Northgate, Cleckheaton, from Parkside, *c.* 1905. The West Riding Union Bank building is on the extreme right.

Northgate, Cleckheaton, *c.* 1905. The Bon Marché millinery shop is on the corner with Cheapside. On the other corner and stretching into Cheapside, are the premises of E.S. Sugden, printer, lithographer and bookbinder. The presence of men and lads in working clothes suggests a midday dinner break from nearby workplaces.

Northgate, Cleckheaton, *c.* 1932, looking towards Lion Stores. The business was started by John Wesley Hillard when he opened a shop on this site in 1885. By the early 1930s, there were about fifty similar retail outlets, many of them in the Spen Valley. In the early 1960s, the name reverted to Hillards and the shops became supermarkets. They were eventually taken over or closed.

Northgate, Cleckheaton, *c.* 1970. This is the same stretch of road as above, but looking in the opposite direction.

Bradford Road, Cleckheaton, with two trams visible, *c.* 1908. Near the skyline on the extreme left is part of the Town Hall. The foreground is dominated by various parts of the George Hotel. The George developed from a coaching inn called the Nag's Head.

Market Place, Cleckheaton, *c.* 1905. This was the second site for the market, the first having been in Town Hall Square. Also shown here are the George Hotel, left, and the main premises of the Cleckheaton Industrial Co-operative Society, erected in 1868, on the right. The market is now held in Horncastle Street.

Cleckheaton Feast in 1908, viewed from the top of Central Methodist Chapel. The fair had developed from a livestock and trading event into an amusement and entertainment one, as the photograph shows. After 1912, the fairground site was converted to a small park.

Cleckheaton Feast, 1905. The travelling fair, with roundabouts, swings and sideshows, including stuffed or pickled freakish animals, attracted large crowds. It seems it was customary for fair-goers to don their best clothes.

Providence Place, Bradford Road, Cleckheaton, in 1902. In the distance is Providence Place Congregational Chapel. Shortly after this photograph was taken, laying of tram tracks commenced.

Balme Road, Cleckheaton, c. 1905. The steep road led to the River Spen and several mills, including Balme, Brookhouse, Moorland and Waterfield Mills. The sign in the centre is for the Water Lane Mills of William Sugden & Sons. Originally founded in 1869, the firm began making shirts in 1896 and moved into Water Lane Mills in 1899.

Pyenot Hall Lane, Cleckheaton, looking towards Greenside and Central Methodist Chapel, 1910. Construction of stylish terrace houses such as these was fairly widespread in the period 1890-1915. Pyenot is believed to be a corruption of a local family name, Pygott.

St Peg Lane, Cleckheaton, photographed from near the entrance to St Peg Mills (left), c. 1910. The sturdy stone-built houses, in almost new condition, have shaped lintels above the windows and dripstones over the doorways. The dripstones, decorative as well as utilitarian, were a throwback to the seventeenth century.

Whitcliffe Road, Cleckheaton, and Booth Street, left, *c.* 1912. At the corner shop, advertisements for ales and stout are more prominent than those for chocolate and cocoa. The shop probably sold most of the popular consumables and provided some kind of delivery service – note the boy with the basket.

Whitcliffe Road, Cleckheaton, *c.* 1912, with the Wesleyan Chapel looming above the other buildings. The gable-ended structure directly above the row of houses is the Drill Hall, built in 1892.

Whitcliffe Mount, Cleckheaton, 1912, with South Parade, left. Beyond the trees of the Turnsteads Estate, right, is Whitcliffe Mount School, newly opened in 1910.

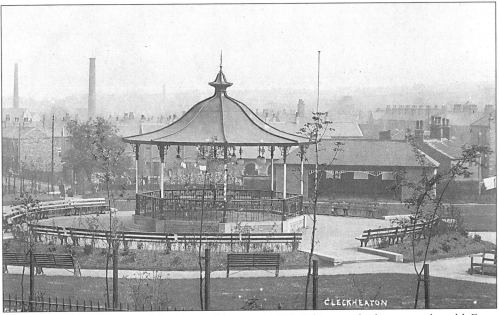

King Edward VII Memorial Park, Cleckheaton, 1913. This was laid out on the old Feast Ground. It was opened on 21 June 1913. Cleckheaton Victoria was just one of the bands which performed in the bandstand, until it was replaced by the War Memorial.

The old cemetery in Whitcliffe Road, Cleckheaton, showing the mortuary chapel. This cemetery was established in 1852. When a new cemetery was opened on Whitechapel Road in 1903, some interments still took place in the old one for many years. The nearest grave on this picture shows that Mrs Amelia Waring died on 27 February 1909.

The new cemetery, Whitechapel Road, Cleckheaton. This photograph was taken shortly after the 1903 opening. Apart from the mortuary chapel, saplings are visible, but no graves.

Bottomley Woodcock, monumental mason. He worked from these premises in Whitechapel Road, Cleckheaton, conveniently sited opposite the gates of the new cemetery. The pair of Waring family graves illustrated on the previous page were made by Woodcock. When the new cemetery was opened, a brochure of rules and regulations, with scales of charges, was issued by Cleckheaton Urban District Council. Plots of land for single graves, each measuring 9ft by 4ft, cost £1, £2, £3 or £5, depending on whether they were marked white, purple, yellow or blue on the plan. A double space cost £1 15s, £3 10s, £5 or £8. Plots marked pink were special and cost even more. These prices took no account of excavation or any other fees. There was a scale of charges for planting upon graves by council workmen. For example, if set out with herbaceous plants, the cost was 3s 6d per year or £3 10s in perpetuity.

North Bierley Joint Hospital for Infectious Diseases, Bradford Road, Cleckheaton, 1903. At this time, catching diphtheria, scarlet fever, smallpox or other infectious diseases probably meant spending several weeks of strict isolation in this hospital. It was erected in 1892; a new wing and mortuary were added in 1898. The hospital was administered by Bradford City and Cleckheaton and Hunsworth Urban District Councils.

Cleckheaton ambulance, early 1900s. The family medicine box with its camphorated oil, olive oil, syrups of figs, flowers of sulphur and kaolin was no match for infectious diseases. Lucky were the people who were never whisked away in the 'fever van'.

Public Baths, Tofts Road, Cleckheaton, *c.* 1905, viewed from the L&YR station. Built by the old Cleckheaton Local Board in 1889, they incorporated swimming baths plus slipper, shower and vapour baths. The caretaker's quarters are on the left. The baths closed in 1974 and were demolished in 1979. The new Spenborough Swimming Pool opened in March 1969.

Fern Bank, Whitcliffe Road, Cleckheaton. The photograph, taken on Thursday 19 October 1905, shows Henry Harrison with the wife and daughter of his son Lawton. The house was occupied in the 1920s and 1930s by William Pearson.

West Riding Union Bank, Market Street, Cleckheaton, *c.* 1912. It was erected in 1898 but, by the time this photograph was taken, it had become the Lancashire & Yorkshire Bank, with the upper rooms occupied by several businesses, including Cadman, Grylls & Cadman, solicitors.

The Liberal Club in Northgate, Cleckheaton, *c.* 1903. Using ashlar stone, it was built in 1897 at a cost of £3,750. It included two billiard rooms, a news room and a large lecture and recreation room capable of holding 200 people.

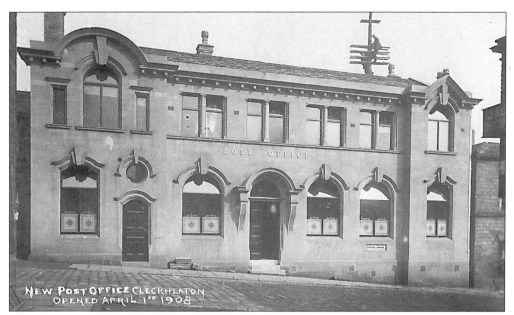

Post Office, Albion Street, Cleckheaton. It is pictured shortly after its ceremonial opening on 1 April 1908. Previously, postal business was transacted from various shops in the town. In 1966, when the Albion Street premises became inadequate, they were replaced by the new General Post Office on the site of the former Central Methodist Chapel.

Albion Street, Cleckheaton, c. 1950, with the Post Office on the left. Just visible on the right is one of the bakery shops of Watson's of Liversedge.

Lower Blacup Farm, Cleckheaton, c. 1905. The buildings date from the seventeenth century and were for many years the home of Thomas Wright, a local writer (1736-1797). Having married Lydia Birkhead at Gretna Green, Thomas settled at Lower Blacup Farm. He was appointed as collector of land tax and window money by local ratepayers and, having collected £80, he placed it in a small drawer of a desk near the door. A collier's wife who lived next door entered and stole £30 in his absence. This and other traumatic experiences caused Thomas, who was a widow by then, to woo, wed and find solace with Alicia Pinder, aged fifteen, of nearby Upper Blacup Farm.

Land's Farm, Roundhill, Cleckheaton, 1915. The farmhouse (not shown), along with those at nearby Mazebrook and Egypt, is believed to date from the seventeenth century. The wooden yoke is being used to carry two buckets of (probably) water.

Scholes Lane, Scholes, 1903. The distant cart is passing Prospect Mills, left. Ahead, beyond the chimney, are Albert Mills. Silk finishing and worsted spinning respectively were carried out in these buildings. In the far distance is the Parish Church of St Philip and St James, built in 1877. Nearer the camera, partly hidden, is the United Methodist Free Chapel of 1879, demolished in 1970.

C.I.C.S SCHOLES LANE END

Cleckheaton Industrial Co-operative Society, branch No. 7, at Scholes Lane End in Scholes, *c.* 1910. The two-horse cart was probably used for wholesale deliveries to the shop in addition to distributing customers' groceries.

Cleckheaton Co-op, branch No. 7, Scholes, *c.* 1910. The manager and his assistant pause from their butter patting and bacon slicing. The store stocked drapery as well as groceries.

Two

Heckmondwike

Market Place, Heckmondwike, 1904. The drinking fountain was erected by public subscription in 1863 to commemorate the marriage of the Prince of Wales – later King Edward VII. The clock, by Potts of Leeds, was added in early 1904, again by public subscription. Shortly after this photograph was taken in June 1904, a small protective wall with railings was built around the foot of the fountain to deter vandals.

Market Place, Heckmondwike, 1906. This was a starting place for horse-drawn carriages, the best known operator being Fred Oade, whose livery stables were in nearby Oldfield Lane. Some small boys appear to be trying to scale the railings around the fountain.

Market Place, Heckmondwike, c. 1925. By then the fountain was purely a decorative feature, although the clock still served a useful purpose. A sign outside Wallace's multiple grocers advertises best Danish butter at 1s 10d per pound.

Market Place, Heckmondwike, *c.* 1905. An open market was started in 1810. In 1866, it was decided to pave the Market Place and its approaches and provide uniform stalls. The new market opened on Saturday 29 February 1868. Traders eventually chose to have a Tuesday as well as a Saturday market.

Market Place, Heckmondwike, *c.* 1960. Locally well-known shop names adorn this picture, some now vanished into history. On the left are Greenwoods the outfitters and Jessops the tailors. To the right is the shop of John S. Driver, grocer.

Market Street, Heckmondwike, *c.* 1903, looking towards the Market Place. On the left (near the lamp) is the Duke William public house; in the distance on the right is the Woodman Inn. These were just two of several pubs in or near the Market Place.

Market Street, Heckmondwike, *c.* 1908. On the right, at the corner with Kay Street, is the Post Office. This served the town until 1983, when the new General Post Office was opened nearby.

Market Street, Heckmondwike, *c.* 1908. Beck Lane is on the left. Thomas Hull was a tailor and hosier at No. 25 (the second shop from the left, with the decorative sign) when 'made to measure' was more popular than it is today.

Westgate, Heckmondwike, *c.* 1960, showing the approach to the Market Place. Raymond Law, decorator, displays an eye for business, while the Pavilion cinema in the distance is nearing the end of its days.

The Green, Heckmondwike, *c.* 1913. In 1912, by public subscription, this barren area was transformed into a small park to commemorate the Coronation of King George V in 1911. In the background on the right is the pork butchering department of Heckmondwike Co-op.

The central stores of the Heckmondwike Co-operative Society and the Green, *c.* 1913. The society was founded in 1860. After using various rented premises in the town, the above stores were erected in 1869. They were soon extended to the left, thus destroying the symmetry of the façade. Numerous branch shops were opened within a radius of four miles. In about 1920, a further block of premises was obtained in Westgate, opposite the parent building. At that time, the 'divvy' was 2s in the pound.

The Green, Heckmondwike, *c.* 1918. It was also known as Green Park. Surrounded by mills, shops and houses, it was a haven in a busy town. Kilburns, whose garage is visible at the far side, were proprietors of the Ideal coaches and charabancs. Their other garage was in Beck Lane.

The War Memorial on the Green, Heckmondwike. In the form of a granite cross, it was unveiled on 27 May 1922 by Cllr J. Parker, Chairman of the Council. The panels at the base show the names of 157 men who sacrificed their lives in the First World War.

The Green, Heckmondwike, *c.* 1914. The parade of shops along Westgate (right) includes Edward Pollitt, pork butcher. To the right of the tram, and topped by a belfry, is the town's second Blanket Hall. Unfortunately the deteriorating condition of the building resulted in its eventual demolition.

High Street, Heckmondwike, *c.* 1960. This is the eastern approach to the Market Place, with the Pavilion Cinema on the left. Symptomatic of the times are the white lines and studs in the road and the car park sign.

Pavilion Cinema, High Street, Heckmondwike. It opened in January 1914 with films and variety turns and closed in December 1962. With staff and patrons posed outside, it is shown here in full glory in the early 1920s. The town's other cinema, the Palace in Croft Street, was begun by Walter Goodall of Liversedge in April 1911, but its use switched to bingo in the mid-1960s. Before these venues were built, animated pictures were shown at the local public baths. Many people made a habit of going to the local cinema once or twice a week. The Saturday matinées were popular with children. The Pavilion possessed a grand pipe organ. The Palace had a Mustal organ and, for a time, an orchestra. Serenade as well as screen!

High Street, Heckmondwike, *c.* 1905. The terrace houses were then relatively new. The tram is bound for Dewsbury. A horse and cart laden with bales descends towards the centre of Heckmondwike.

The Junction, Heckmondwike, *c.* 1908. This scene, captured from the end of Halifax Road, shows the same terrace houses as the top picture and, in the distance, Upper Independent Chapel. The lines in the foreground carried trams to and from Dewsbury.

The Junction, Heckmondwike, *c*. 1906. Here, High Street ends; the road diverges into Batley Road (left) and Halifax Road (right) where a tram is heading for Dewsbury. The children, some of them wearing clogs, appear to be in no danger. At extreme left is a Lion grocery store, also visible in the previous picture.

Walkley Lane, Heckmondwike, with Station Lane on the right, *c*. 1910. The small confectionery and off-license shop was patronised by railway travellers and local people. In the centre of the photograph (on Walkley Lane) is the Public Library, erected in 1907. The site was given by Sir Thomas Firth; the buildings were provided through the Carnegie Trust.

Victoria Street, Heckmondwike, *c.* 1908. Victoria Street Infants School and St Saviour's Church are in the distance. The houses, mostly dating from around 1895 or earlier, look well-built, in contrast to the road and pavements. Some of those on the right were erected as back-to-back type with rear yards and shared dry privies. Windows of cellars are discernible at causeway level. Cellars were used for storing perishables, also coal which was shovelled down through horizontal or vertical cavities, normally covered with a cast plate.

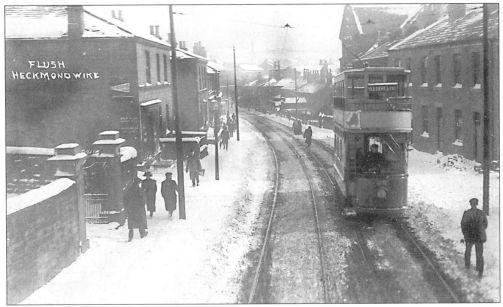

Westgate, Flush, Heckmondwike. Pedestrians and tram (photographed from another tram) seem unhampered by the wintry conditions. The tramcar, on its way to Liversedge and Cleckheaton, has just passed Westgate Congregational Chapel.

Three
Liversedge

Station Road, Millbridge, *c*. 1906. Millbridge was the industrial heart of Liversedge. A corn mill had existed there since medieval times. Station Road, actually part of Halifax Road, led to the now-vanished station. On the left of this picture are the premises of George Simpson & Son, tanners and curriers. To the right are John Street and Spring Street.

Station Road, Millbridge, *c.* 1906. On the corner of Valley Road is Fred Kaye's grocery and off-licence shop. In the distance, behind the nearest tall chimney, is the old corn mill.

Station Road, Millbridge, *c.* 1906. In the centre distance is the old corn mill, not the original but one most likely erected in the late eighteenth century. Corn milling probably ceased there in the 1880s, after which the building was occupied by a variety of traders, including a hair merchant.

Station Road, Millbridge, early 1920s. This photograph, taken in the opposite direction to the two previous ones, shows demolition of the old corn mill, although the chimney is still intact.

Station Road, Millbridge, early 1920s. These lockup shops were situated near the old corn mill. At various times, they were occupied by a hairdresser, cobbler, motor engineer and grocer. In the 1920s, Mrs Emily Oldham was newsagent and tobacconist at No. 4 Station Road, shown here on the right. She also sold postcards and stamps. The mill visible in the background had stood adjacent to the old corn mill.

Millbridge Working Men's Club, Huddersfield Road. The photograph was taken in April 1913, shortly before the building was demolished and replaced by a new structure on the same site. Flat caps, some bowler hats and a few alberts (watches on waistcoats) are much in evidence.

Huddersfield Road, looking towards Leeds Road, Millbridge, *c.* 1925. On the extreme left is the Millbridge Working Men's Club, built in 1914. Further down are the Wesleyan Methodist Chapel (now demolished) and Lion Stores. In the distance on the right is part of the carpet manufacturing complex of Samuel Cooke.

Millbridge Park. This scene was recorded within a few days of the park being opened between Halifax Road and Huddersfield Road on 4 August 1928. It shows flower beds, shrubs, tennis courts, a bowling green, a pavilion and toilets. Some of the buildings on the right are part of the Cooke mill.

Swan Crossroads, Liversedge, c. 1907. The single-storey block of shops was eventually extended upwards to provide first-floor accommodation, but all the buildings shown were later demolished, as was the Swan Hotel, which gave the crossroads its name. Overhead wires and tram tracks form interesting patterns; the single track on the right traversed Leeds Road before turning left into Gomersal Road.

Frost Hill, Liversedge, *c.* 1903. John Frost, a local farmer gave his name to the hill. On the right of this picture, next to the newsagents, is Fred Blackburn's shop. For many years, he was the town's best-known watch and clock maker and he later went into the cycle trade.

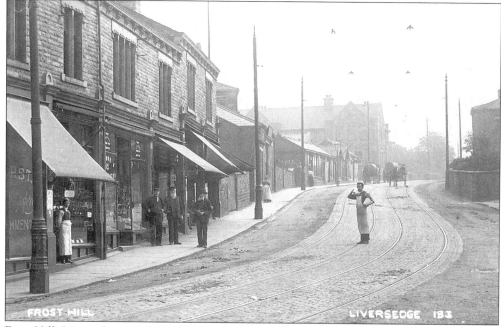

Frost Hill, Liversedge, *c.* 1905. At the top of the hill, beyond the two water carts is the head office and depot of the Yorkshire (Woollen District) Electric Tramways Co. Observe the man imbibing in the road.

Water Gate, Littletown, *c.* 1905. Listing Lane (Gomersal Lane) is on the right. Beyond the small roundabout is the Old Oak Inn. Most of the other buildings were obliterated for road widening and a dual carriageway in the early 1960s, when Water Gate became part of Bradford Road.

Water Gate, Littletown, *c.* 1912. The tram, passing the Old Oak Inn and bound for Cleckheaton, is about to transfer from single to double track. Beyond the drapery and millinery shop of A.E. Lawford are the premises of Fred Drake, hairdresser and tobacconist.

Toll Bar, Liversedge, at the junction of Huddersfield Road and Robert Town Lane, 1906. It was built for the Birstall and Huddersfield Turnpike of 1764-65. A gate, long dismantled, halted vehicles, whose drivers were obliged to pay a toll for road upkeep. The windowed multi-sided projection gave good visibility along the roads.

Huddersfield Road, Liversedge, c. 1937. The gap between the houses denotes the bridge over the railway. On the left is Union Road, with a fish and chip shop on the corner.

Liversedge Hall Lane seen from Huddersfield Road, 1920s. The hall, further along the road, was built in about 1600. A number of other elegant houses were erected in the area, including Fieldhurst, behind the trees beyond the road sweeper.

Corn Mill Lane, Liversedge, *c.* 1910. It was known as Little Lane up to around 1900. There was a mill in the vicinity, partly used for corn grinding. In the distance, extreme left, is one of the gasometers of the Heckmondwike & Liversedge Gas Co. This came under the aegis of Spenborough Council in 1921.

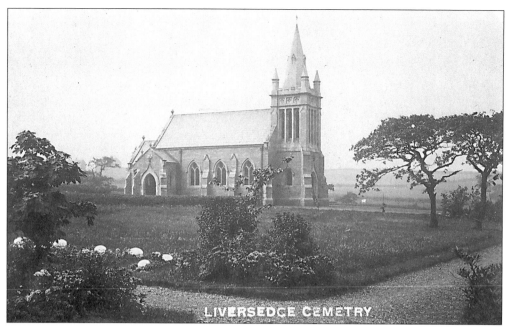

Cemetery, Clough Lane, Liversedge. Covering twelve acres, this was established by Liversedge Urban District Council in 1903. The grounds and mortuary chapel are depicted shortly after their inauguration.

Cemetery lodge, Liversedge. In pristine condition, the lodge and gateway look splendidly spiritual as well as modish. Ladies' and gentlemen's conveniences are visible at left and right respectively.

Halifax Road, Hightown Heights, *c.* 1920. The road originated as part of the Halifax to Wakefield turnpike route. The Liberal Club is on the right. The chimney behind the houses formed part of the Victoria Dye Works of Harrison, Gardner & Co.

The Post Office, Robert Town Lane, Robert Town, *c.* 1908. Postmaster Charles Fisher stands at the entrance of his shop and residence. He sold everything from a postcard to a packet of tea, from chocolate to children's hoops. Some, now vanished, papers and periodicals are placarded, as is Dr Beatty, whose board proclaims that he calls daily to collect messages.

Grey Ox Inn, Hartshead Lane, Hartshead, c. 1905. At the time, the pub-cum-farm sold eggs, milk and beer from the barrel. Hartshead village is visible in the distance; set on high ground, it had two dozen farms at the beginning of the twentieth century.

Springwell Cottage, Forge Lane, Norristhorpe, c. 1910. The house, with cellar and attic, was occupied by George Spurr, a joiner, builder and undertaker. Many families, insisting on a good 'send off' for their loved one, had problems paying funeral expenses. Apart from undertaker's fees, there was the expenditure of mourning clothes, providing a ham tea and so on.

56

Four

Gomersal
and Beyond

 LL HOTEL GOMERSALL

Bull's Head, Little Gomersal, c. 1922. Situated at the junction of Lower Lane with Listing Lane, it dates back to the late 1700s. The middle portion was probably used as a blacksmith's workshop. The landlord in the early 1920s was Squire Bentley. By the late 1920s, it was managed by the Wood family.

Oxford Road, Gomersal, *c.* 1922. Fred Midgley's confectionery shop is visible on the left, while slightly lower down is Joseph Preston's pianoforte shop. The cricket field is off the picture to the right.

Joseph Preston, pianoforte dealer, Oxford Road, Gomersal, *c.* 1912. In addition to selling, repairing and tuning pianos, Mr Preston sold sheet music and postcards. He lived on the premises and served as registrar of births, marriages and deaths for Gomersal. The net curtains were an attempt to deter prying passengers on the upper decks of trams.

Oxford Road, Gomersal, *c.* 1925. The photograph was taken looking towards Hill Top and the White Horse Inn. The children are Cyril Duce and Donald Swailes.

Oxford Road, Hill Top, Gomersal, *c.* 1948. Church Lane is on the right, between the trees and cigarette booth. Beyond the lane is the White Horse Inn.

White Horse Inn, Hill Top. Gomersal, *c.* 1924. This nineteenth-century building replaced an earlier hostelry. It is pictured near the intersection of two old turnpike roads – Oxford Road and Spen Lane/Church Lane.

Oxford Road, Hill Top, Gomersal, *c.* 1922. On the right, at the end of Spen Lane (also known as Elland Road) is one of four stores of the Gomersal Industrial Co-operative Society, the others being on Oxford Road in Great Gomersal, on Moor Lane and on Drub Lane in Birkenshaw. All these shops were absorbed by the Cleckheaton Industrial Co-operative Society in about 1930.

Oxford Road and Lower Lane, Great Gomersal, *c.* 1912. Within the junction is one of the Gomersal Industrial Co-operative Society stores. Lower Lane (later Knowles Lane) on the right was part of the original road through Gomersal. The bowler-hatted man has just passed the Shoulder of Mutton Inn, which was built in the eighteenth century, but has since been altered. When this photograph was taken, and for many years after, the Wilby family were landlords.

Oxford Road, Great Gomersal. The Gomersal Co-op shop is on the right. The scene was recorded sometime before 13 October 1903, the date when trams commenced operating a public service from Dewsbury to Birkenshaw. This must be a trial run.

Lower Lane, Little Gomersal, *c.* 1910. Beyond the sharp right-hand bend in the road, there used to be a dryhouse for drying wool or cloth.

Heckmondwike & District Co-operative Society, Branch No. 8, Upper Lane, Little Gomersal, *c.* 1928. When the society grew and encroached on the territory of other societies, 'district' was added to the name. The purpose-built butchering van, seen centre, plied the streets selling meat and offal, and boosting the customer's dividend!

Spen Lane, Hill Top, Gomersal, 1910. Just to the right of centre, partly hidden by the wall, is the Post Office; to its left a branch of the London Joint City & Midland Bank. At extreme right is the lodge of Hill Top House.

Pollard Hall, Gomersal, c. 1928. To the left of the four original gables (two of which may date from before 1630) is the late Victorian extension, which replaced a group of industrial buildings. In 1752, the Burnley family moved into Pollard Hall, which they purchased in 1843 along with Gomersal Mills. William Burnley started his textile business in part of the hall before moving to the mills, which are visible in the background.

Mechanics' Institute, Oxford Road, Gomersal, *c.* 1910. It was erected in 1851 and enlarged in 1890. Equipped with a lecture room and library, it provided non-religious education, mainly for adults who aspired to better themselves. The building eventually became the Public Hall.

Oakroyd Lodge, Birkenshaw, *c.* 1910. Situated on the west side of Bradford Road, this led to Oakroyd Hall and its extensive grounds. In 1964, the new headquarters and training school of the West Riding Fire Service were established on the site.

Bradford Road, Birkenshaw with the headquarters of the Birkenshaw Industrial Society, *c.* 1906. From left to right: the office, butchering, footwear and grocery departments.

Bradford Road, Birkenshaw, *c.* 1950. This illustration shows the same stretch of road as the top view. The George Fourth public house has a sign for Ramsden's Stone Trough Ales (of Halifax). An arrow points to the railway station up Town Street (right) which closed in 1953.

The Green, East Bierley, *c*. 1932. Of uncertain origin, the stocks on the triangular village green were more of a novelty than a form of punishment when this photograph was taken. In the background, on South View Road, is Joe Mitchell's grocery shop and post office.

Cleckheaton Road, Oakenshaw, *c*. 1905. Richardson Street and Back Richardson Street are on the left. Many of the villagers worked at the worsted mill shown in the middle distance. Some of the children pictured were probably destined to become 'part-timers' there.

Five
Churches and Chapels

Cleckheaton St Luke's AFC, 1913/14 season. Second team members stand proudly outside the church. Amateur soccer (and rugby) clubs existed throughout the Spen Valley, some of them supported by local churches and chapels.

St Peter's Church, Hartshead, before 1881. In that year, the building was heavily restored, although the Norman tower was retained. Patrick Brontë was curate there at the time of the Luddite troubles. *Shirley*, written by his daughter Charlotte, contains references to the Spen Valley.

St Peter's Church, Hartshead, c. 1912. On 25 June and 2 July 1927, the Hartshead and Kirklees Pageant was staged in a field near Freak Field Lane. It was a presentation of village life around Hartshead through the ages, with proceeds for the church and Sunday school. 'Cars and charas to be parked in next field. Yorkshire buses between Elland, Clifton, Hartshead and Cleckheaton pass the grounds' – from the event's programme.

St John's Church, Church Street, Cleckheaton, *c.* 1912. It was erected in 1830 and enlarged in 1864. The sculptured stone reredos behind the altar, depicting the Last Supper, was added in 1883. The oak screen and pulpit were presented in 1910. Of special interest are the many biblical extracts painted above and at the sides of the chancel arch.

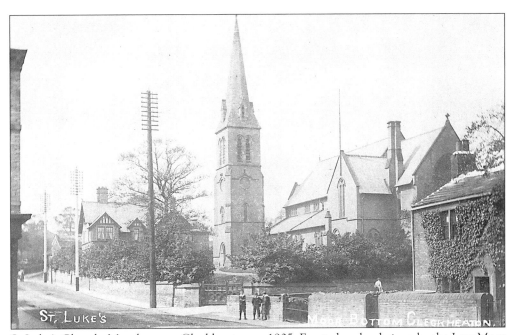

St Luke's Church, Moorbottom, Cleckheaton, *c.* 1905. Erected on land given by the Low Moor Iron Co., it was consecrated in 1889, replacing a temporary church on the same site. The unusually-positioned tower received its clock in 1913.

St James's Church, Church Street, Heckmondwike, *c.* 1910. Gothic in style, it was erected in 1831, partly to compensate for a lack of churches in certain areas. The Sunday school is visible on the opposite side of the road.

Whit Monday procession, Heckmondwike, 1911. Beneath a sunny sky, children from the Parish Church of St James and St Saviour's Church parade through the Market Place. Many of the girls are wearing their new clothes, traditionally brought out at that time of year.

Whit Monday service, Heckmondwike, 1913. The Whitsuntide celebrations always included hymn singing and processions. Here, in the grounds of St James's vicarage, children and adults prepare to sing. Banners used in the parade are displayed at the back.

Boy Scouts, Heckmondwike, Whit Monday, 1911. The Whit procession was usually followed by tea, games and sports. The St Saviour's scouts pause for a photograph during entertainment in St James's vicarage grounds.

'Ye Old Village Wedding' by Hightown Parish Church ladies' sewing party, 29 November 1913. This presentation, with slight variations, was popular around the Spen Valley. Apart from a bride and groom, the characters, usually all played by the fairer sex, included a policeman and schoolmaster. On this occasion, a few boys were recruited.

'Ye Old Village Wedding' at Hightown Parish Church, 1913. The five village gossips pose with the nurse. The Parish Church of St Barnabas, seen in the background, was built in 1893.

Moravian Sunday School,
⇛ GOMERSAL. ⇚

The Young Men's Class beg to announce their SECOND

Annual CONCERT

to be held

On Saturday, January 10th, 1914.

Doors open at 6-30. Concert to commence at 7 o'clock

ARTISTES—

Soprano ... Miss H. TAYLOR, Drighlington.

Mezzo Soprano and Violinist Miss D. MYCOCK, Gomersal.

Contralto ... Miss E. SHAW, Bradford.

Tenor ... ... Mr. H. FURNESS, Gomersal.

Baritone and Elocutionist Mr. G. HEPWORTH,
Ravensthorpe.

Elocutionist Miss C. WEAVER, Heckmondwike.

Humorist ... Mr. W. RUSHWORTH, Gomersal.

Comic Dialogue Messrs. R. WEAVER & F. HUGHES,
Heckmondwike.

Accompanist Miss EVELYN WOOD, Liversedge.

Dialogue ... ... MEMBERS OF THE CLASS.

Admission—ADULTS, 6d. CHILDREN, 4d.

Tickets may be had from Members of the Class, or from
H. FURNESS, Secretary and Treasurer.

Proceeds in Aid of School Funds.

E. Smith, Printer, Little Gomersal.

Moravian Sunday School, Gomersal. This is the front of the programme for the annual concert. The Moravians, a German Protestant sect, established a settlement at Little Gomersal in 1751, between Upper and Lower Lanes and near Quarry Road. Pioneers in education, they had previously founded a settlement at Fulneck in 1743.

Providence Place Congregational Chapel, Cleckheaton, c. 1950. 'Spen Valley has often been called the metropolis of dissent, and perhaps there is no district in England in which Nonconformity embraces such a large proportion of the population within its fold.' So wrote Frank Peel at the beginning of his book *Nonconformity in the Spen Valley* published in 1891. (Peel's better-known book *Spen Valley Past and Present*, which contains some Nonconformist history, was published in 1893 and reprinted in 1987.) The Church of England had never become firmly established in the Spen Valley. The exceptions were the Anglican churches at Hartshead and Whitechapel, which served the whole area. From the eleventh century to the early nineteenth century, no new Anglican churches were erected in the Spen Valley. The early Dissenters or Nonconformists met in houses, often in secret. Many of them became known as Independents or Congregationalists. They started building places specifically for worship and fellowship. Then came the evangelical revival, led by John Wesley, the founder of Methodism. Between them, the Independents and Methodists captured the imagination of the Spen Valley people. Imposing chapels were replaced by finer and bigger ones. Intentionally, they were designed to look dissimilar to Anglican churches. Providence Place Congregational Chapel (later United Reformed) is a typical example. It was built between 1857 and 1859 on the site of an earlier chapel. The arcaded façade, with Corinthian columns and a stepped approach, is more redolent of a town hall than a place of worship.

Providence Place Congregational Chapel, Cleckheaton, 1904. Its 1,500 seats were often occupied by a thronging congregation. Underneath the main building were rooms for Sunday school and other uses. The tercentenary was celebrated in 1972, but the chapel closed as a place of worship in 1992.

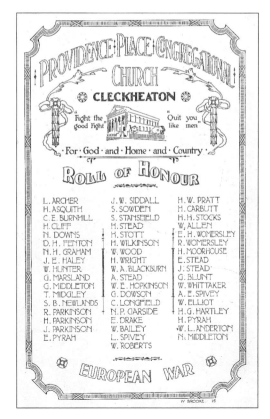

Providence Place Congregational Chapel, Cleckheaton. This card was issued in memory of those who gave their lives in the First World War.

Upper Independent Chapel (Congregational), High Street, Heckmondwike, c. 1925. The design, by local architect Arthur A. Scott, specified a façade with a pair of dissimilar domed turrets, joined by a pedimented portico with four Corinthian columns. When the chapel opened in 1890, the total amount collected at the various inaugural celebrations was £1,441.

Upper Independent Chapel, High Street, Heckmondwike, 1905. In front of the rostrum-style pulpit is a semicircular communion rail, a pattern continued through to the box pews. The horseshoe-shaped gallery is supported on fluted iron columns. The back of this postcard includes the message, 'Do you like this? We only go on wet days.'

Grove Congregatioal Chapel, Oxford Road, Gomersal, *c*. 1925. It was built in 1825-26 on land given by James Burnley, a prominent local Congregationalist. The uncluttered but impressive front contrasts sharply with the façades of some of the later town chapels.

Wesleyan Methodist Chapel, Latham Lane, *c*. Gomersal, 1905. The Gomersal Wesleyan society evolved from the one at Birstall. In 1827, Edward Brooke of Honley was invited to conduct their anniversary services. The afternoon service was held in a field; the evening one in Grove Chapel. During the services, Mr Brooke decided to donate £50 towards the erection of a chapel. Further contributions were forthcoming. The new building, pictured above, was opened on 20 June 1827. The unusual curved front is flanked by two wings, with doors to the galleried interior.

Wesleyan Methodist Chapel, Whitcliffe Road, Cleckheaton, *c.* 1907. Various other branches of the Methodist Church, including the Primitive Methodists, sprang from the original Wesleyan Methodist Church, which was founded by John Wesley. In 1932, Methodist Union brought most of the factions together. In Victorian and Edwardian days, many people in the Spen Valley were drawn to the chapels of Nonconformity, particularly the Congregational and multifarious Methodist ones, which managed to combine the cosy-club atmosphere with strict rules on drink and gambling. Activities were not confined to Sunday, when two religious services and two sessions of Sunday school were normal. Midweek activities included class meetings, Sisterhood and Brotherhood meetings, choir practices and the Band of Hope. Annual events were the Sunday school prize giving and concert, the school anniversary and Whit walk and perhaps a performance of the *Messiah*. There were cricket clubs and sewing circles, bazaars and charabanc trips. At chapel, many young people met their future spouses. The above chapel, typically Victorian in appearance, was opened in 1889. It replaced an earlier Wesleyan Chapel, built in Northgate in 1853, which had rapidly become too small. Beneath the larger chapel in Whitcliffe Road were a large schoolroom, designed to accommodate 1,000 children, and 13 other rooms for various activities. The chapel closed in 1966 and was demolished later. The remaining congregation transferred to Central Chapel.

Wesleyan Chapel, Whitcliffe Road, Cleckheaton, *c.* 1907. The chapel, with its gallery, was capable of seating 1,000 persons. Visible behind the pulpit are choir stalls, while in front, the curvature of the communion rail is carried through to the pews, thus ensuring that everyone faced the preacher.

Whit Monday gathering, 28 May 1912. Outside the Wesleyan Chapel in Whitcliffe Road, Cleckheaton, a few of the Sunday school's 316 children pause for the photographer. About ten Cleckheaton Sunday schools had their own parade on the day, with stops for hymn singing, followed by a tea and bun 'tuck-in' and sports in various fields.

Central Chapel, Cleckheaton, *c.* 1950. Opened in 1879, it became known as the Cathedral of Free Methodism. It belonged to the United Methodist Free Church, another branch of Methodism. Pevsner described the building as 'amazingly pompous'. The giant portico was flanked by two decorated domed towers. The Sunday school on the left was built in 1897. The congregation used it for worship from 1959 onwards. The chapel was demolished in 1961.

Central Chapel, Cleckheaton, *c.* 1905. The architect was Mr Reuben Castle of Cleckheaton. The lavishly decorated interior, seating 1,764 people, complemented the exterior. Worthy of particular note are the large pulpit and decorative organ, with figures. In the 1880s, an 80-strong group carried out house visitation and helped the minister with outdoor preaching.

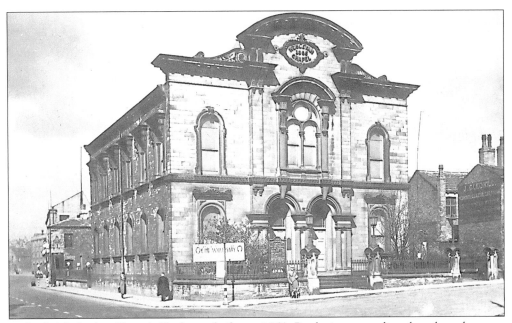

Parkside Methodist Chapel, Heckmondwike, *c.* 1950. Replacing an earlier chapel on the same site near the Green, this former Wesleyan Chapel was opened in 1866, still with a debt lying over it. This debt was finally cleared in 1878 when a big bazaar was held. The chapel closed in 1959 and was later pulled down.

Wesleyan Methodist Chapel, Far Common Road, Robert Town, *c.* 1905. Built in 1839, its austere exterior looks fairly typical of country Methodism at that time. A Sunday school was erected behind the chapel in 1926, replacing an earlier one in Church Road. The chapel was demolished in 1968, when the congregation moved into the Sunday school.

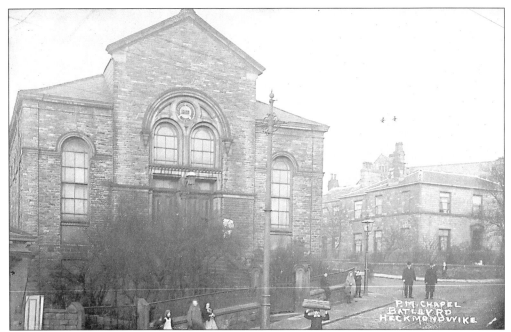

Primitive Methodist Chapel, Batley Road, Heckmondwike, *c.* 1908. Early Heckmondwike Primitives worshipped in a small chapel vacated by the Methodist New Connection (another Methodist sect). When this became too small, the above chapel was built (actually just over the Batley boundary) at a cost of £2,000. It was opened in 1869, with seating for 500 and ancillary rooms below. It was closed in 1975 and later demolished.

Primitive Methodist Chapel, Halifax Road, Hightown, *c.* 1910. Opened in 1871, it was built near Industrial Street, which is visible beyond the cabins. Closure came in 1969. Hugh Bourne and William Clowes founded the Primitive Methodist Church. Primitive Methodists were tagged as 'glad and tuneful folk' or 'ranters' because of their lively preaching and singing.

Independent Methodist Chapel, Chapel Street, Cleckheaton. Not to be confused with the Independents who became known as Congregationalists, the Independent Methodists retained their separate identity after the 1932 Union. The chapel shown above, which replaced an earlier one, was opened on 22 September 1875.

Demonstration, Heckmondwike & District Band of Hope Union, Saturday 17 August 1912. After a lapse of several years, the event was resurrected in 1912. About 800 children assembled in Greenside for a procession round the town, led by Cleckheaton Temperance Band, followed by a gathering on the football field in Beck Lane. The Heckmondwike Wesleyan contingent is pictured.

HIGHTOWN
WESLEYAN ORCHESTRAL SOCIETY.

Eleventh Concert,

In the SCHOOLROOM,

On Saturday, March 6th, 1920.

Solo 'Cello : **Miss Kathleen Moorhouse**

Cleckheaton.

Soloist : **Mr. Wilfrid Hudson,**

Yeadon.

Orchestra of **30** Performers.

Conductor - - Mr. FRANK SHARP.

Leader and Deputy Conductor - Mr. G. W. CLEMENTS.

Accompanist - Mr. WALTER WOOD.

Doors open at 7-0 p.m.   Commence at 7-30 p.m.

Prices of Admission:—Reserved Seats, **2/4** (including Tax).

Unreserved Seats, **1/3**   do.

(A few only)

TICKETS may be had from the Secretary, Mr. FREDK. WILKINSON, Hightown,

The Globe Printing Company, Liversedge.

Hightown Wesleyan Orchestral Society. This is the front cover of the four-page programme for the concert on 6 March 1920. It included the orchestra playing the *Tannhauser* march by Wagner and Mr Hudson singing *Come to the Fair*. The society was formed in 1908, although its operations were curtailed during the First World War. A concert given by the society on 12 December 1914 raised money for the Belgian Relief Fund.

Six

Schools

Schoolboys, Heckmondwike, *c.* 1888. The British & Foreign Schools Society (founded in 1808) and the National Society (1811) were responsible for providing religious and other teaching for poorer children. The former was an undenominational organization with strong backing from the Nonconformists; the latter was formed by the Church of England. This picture shows boys from a National School (Anglican) in or near Heckmondwike (the exact location is uncertain, but the photographer hailed from the town). The boys are variously dressed, some of them are bow-legged and one appears to need a haircut.

National School, Hill Top, Gomersal, *c.* 1922. It was erected at the top of Church Lane in 1874 and enlarged in 1890 to take 410 children. Its ecclesiastical design is not surprising, considering it was built by the Church of England. The school was destroyed by fire in the 1970s.

Council School, Gomersal, *c.* 1922. It was erected on Oxford Road at Birdacre in 1912 for 250 children. The elementary school leaving age was raised to 13 years in 1880. It was advanced to 14 by the Education Act of 1918, when the half-time system, whereby some children spent half of each day at work, was abolished. It lingered in the Spen Valley, however, for a few more years.

Board School, Bradford Road, Littletown, c. 1910. The Forster Education Act of 1870 made elementary education compulsory and required the setting up of local boards to build schools with money from the rates. The above school was erected in 1878 to accommodate 506 children. The boys' and infants' entrances can be seen at left and right respectively.

Hightown Council School, Halifax Road, c. 1948. The Balfour Education Act of 1902 made local government responsible for elementary and secondary education. Existing board schools became council schools, although the old title lingered to the middle of the century. Hightown Council (formerly Board) School was erected in 1878 for 433 children. The chimney of Victoria Dye Works is visible in the distance.

Higher Grade School, High Street, Heckmondwike, 1905. The Heckmondwike School Board decided in 1894 to erect a secondary school for boys and girls. It opened in 1898 with around 900 pupils, having incorporated several other local schools. As well as academic tuition, the curriculum included technical and commercial training, which had been the metier of the Mechanics' Institute.

Heckmonwike Grammar School. On 6 December 1929, the name of Heckmondwike Higher Grade School was changed to Heckmomdwike Grammar School. At the time, a series of postcards was issued. Above and following are three examples. This one shows the school hall with classrooms either side.

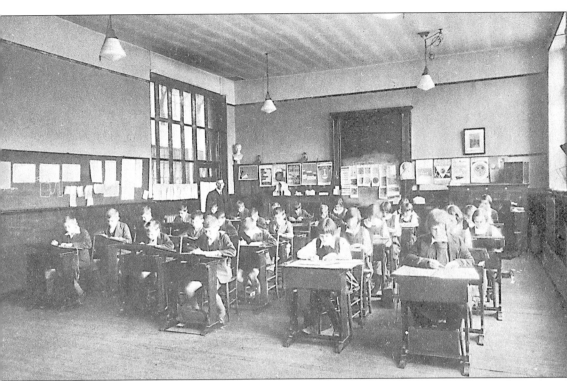

Heckmondwike Grammar School, art room. This is one of the rooms which abutted on to the school hall. Short-trousered boys and gym-slipped girls sit behind desks with adjustable tops.

Heckmondwike Grammar School, domestic room. The room appears to be well-equipped, although some of the apparatus looks dated by today's standards. Many a girl must have looked at the clock on the wall and wondered whether her cake had been in the oven long enough!

Whitcliffe Mount School, Cleckheaton. The school was erected in 1909-10 to a design by Leeds architect W.H. Thorpe. The £20,000 needed for its construction was raised locally without any cost falling on the County Council, the authority then responsible for higher education. It included £5,500 raised by public subscription and private donations, £1,600 from the sale of the former technical school building in Brook Street and the balance from Cleckheaton Urban District Council. The school, which opened as Cleckheaton Technical and Secondary School, is shown with building work nearing completion. Designed to take 300 students, it had spacious well-lit classrooms. The ground floor included a wood and metal workshop, cookery and laundry rooms, a mechanical laboratory, dining room and gymnasium. On the first floor were art and dressmaking rooms, chemistry, biology and physics laboratories and a lecture room. Older ex-pupils may remember having to pass their County Minor Scholarship at age ten, before admission to Whitcliffe Mount Grammar School, as it became known. The school was extensively enlarged in 1958, and also in 1973 when it became the area's comprehensive school.

Seven
Industry and Trade

Flush Mills, Westgate, Heckmondwike, 1903. The original mills were purchased by Edwin Firth in 1822. He was succeeded by his son, Thomas Freeman Firth, in 1863. Disastrous fires in 1846 and 1928 meant that extensive rebuilding was twice necessary. After producing woollen cloth and blankets, T.F. Firth & Sons eventually specialized in carpets, rugs, ladies mantle cloths and imitation furs and skins for motor-travelling rugs. The tram is on a trial run.

John Darnbrook & Sons, wool and waste merchants, Crofts Lane, Heckmondwike, *c.* 1910. The town had over a dozen wool and waste merchants at the time. Woollen rags were placed in bales, similar to the one shown, and sent to auction. The reprocessed wool was mixed with new wool to produce mungo and shoddy for cheap but high quality blankets and rugs.

Arthur Lambert, fellmonger and woolstapler, Union Mills, Beck Lane, Heckmondwike. Workmen are grouped on a dray used for carrying bales of wool, *c.* 1897. The firm was involved in the removal of wool from sheepskins (fellmongering), sorting it and moving it on to manufacturers (woolstapling). Lambert was in business at Union Mills until the mid-1920s. Observe the irons beneath the clogs.

Hearl Heaton & Sons Ltd, Crown Works, Station Road, Liversedge. The firm originated in 1809. It specialized in the manufacture and repair of accessories for the woollen, worsted, cotton and flax industries. These included grinding frames, emery rollers, condenser bobbins and loom spindles. The company now makes cable drums.

John A. & Edwin Lawford, curriers and leather merchants, Spen Valley Leather Works, Liversedge. The top of the firm's invoice, dated 15 June 1937, shows the works, which abutted on to Station Road on the right and Ashton Clough Road in the foreground.

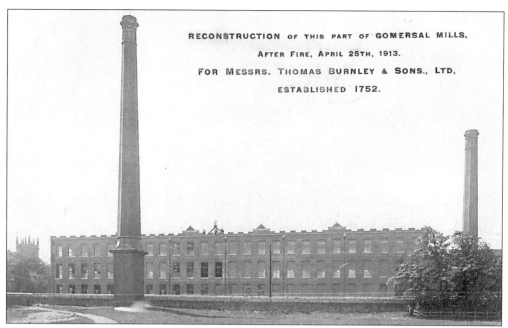

Gomersal Mills. The firm, founded in 1752 by William Burnley, was, by 1913, being managed by three other Burnleys – William, Thomas and Thomas Lockwood. One evening, Thomas was playing billiards in Pollard Hall when, pulling back the curtains, he was alarmed to find Gomersal Mills in flames. About 300 people were thrown out of work. Substantial rebuilding was soon commenced, as depicted above.

Entrance to Gomersal Mills, Spen Lane, c. 1925. The mills specialized in woolcombing (separation of fibres), worsted spinning and dyeing, and produced both weaving and hosiery yarns. Although the firm passed out of Burnley ownership shortly after the rebuild, the Burnley name was retained. Indeed, it has always been known locally as Burnley's Mill.

A decorated wagon belonging to Thomas Burnley & Sons Ltd, laden with various types of wool. The posters, which describe the firm as a manufacturer of Scotch fingering and knitting wools, show the mill after rebuilding which dates the float to after 1913.

Spen Mills and St Peg Mills, Cleckheaton, *c.* 1910. At the time, Firth & Blackburn were millers and maltsters in Spen Mills, seen here at the end of the large Mann Dam. To the right, in St Peg Mills, W. Atkinson & Son, were worsted spinners. Their four-storey buildings had been erected around a hollow square. The River Spen flows quietly by.

Strawberry Bank Colliery, Liversedge, c. 1911. The pit, also known as Liversedge Colliery, was operated by the Liversedge Coal Co., although the Dymond family, coal owners in Bradford and Huddersfield, were responsible for much of its early development. The colliery lasted from approximately 1868 until July 1919. The list of collieries which were once worked in and around Liversedge also includes Millbridge, Primrose Hill, Park Farm, Quaker Lane, Smithy Hill, Southfield, Stanley Main, Tanhouse Mill and Woodside. Towards the end of the nineteenth century there were over fifty working pits throughout the Spen Valley. None of them remain, the last mine to close was Gomersal in June 1973. Strawberry Bank Colliery was situated on the south side of Liversedge, with access from either Huddersfield Road or Headlands Road. The Lancashire & Yorkshire Railway skirted its eastern side and transported much of the output of coal and, later, coke. The coke oven plant was installed in the 1890s, after which most of the mined coal was converted to coke. It was sent to Sheffield, Hull and Manchester. The above photograph shows the timber-framed headgear, with colliers about to descend the shaft. Beyond the headgear are the engine/boiler house and integral chimney. Strawberry Bank Colliery did not survive long enough for any major modernization. The crudeness of the buildings was matched by the austere conditions which the men and boys endured.

Strawberry Bank Colliery, Liversedge, *c*. 1911. The hotchpotch of structures in the colliery yard includes part of the engine house, left, and an air shaft, right. In the distance is a row of colliers' houses known as Dymond Buildings. Some washing is hanging out to dry.

Liversedge Colliery AFC, 1908/09. Sport played an important part in the lives of these colliers. There was also a reserve team.

Strawberry Bank Colliery, *c.* 1911. These are some of the coke ovens, with Headlands Road in the background. Coal was conveyed from the pit head and lifted by a small elevator, left, to the top of the ovens. It was then wheeled in small tubs along tracks, before being tipped through horizontal apertures for processing.

Strawberry Bank Colliery, *c.* 1911. Here, coke oven workers have a breather in front of the ovens depicted in the top view. The product was manually scooped out of the ovens and transferred by wheelbarrows to railway trucks. These were shunted on to the main railway line.

John William Thornton, coal merchant, Liversedge. The vehicle bodywork was built by another local firm, Joseph Ramsden Ltd, motor body builders, Liversedge.

Spen Valley Laundry. The firm was developed from the early 1900s by Robert Pullan. Laundries, which collected and delivered every week, were popular before the days of automatic washers and coin-operated machines. The vehicle is parked at the laundry in Ashton Clough Road, Liversedge; the gas-powering device probably being a First World War expedient.

Tom Hurley, removals contractor, Cleckheaton. The firm operated a fleet of horse and steam propelled vehicles, including this monster from around 1910.

Spenborough Fire Brigade at Cleckheaton in 1920. This Dennis appliance was one of two fire engines purchased by Spenborough UDC in 1919/20. They were particularly necessary for fighting fires at textile mills, which usually contained easily combustible material.

Brunswick Mills, Heckmondwike. The Co-operative Wholesale Society acquired the site and buildings in 1880 for the development of a large boot and shoe manufactory. After adjacent land was procured, more buildings were added in the mid-1890s and the complex assumed the form shown above. The older parts, forming a half-square, are the structures at the rear and on the left, including the gatehouse at the front (on Thomas Street). The newer buildings, forming a complete square, are to the right, abutting on to a row of houses. Hides, mainly from abroad, were received sun-dried, shorn of hair and partially tanned. They underwent further processing at the mills, including trimming, shaving and scouring. Parts of the newer buildings were devoted to actual boot and shoe making, where up to fifty operations were carried out on specialized machines. Boots were made to suit miners, farmers, navvies, quarrymen, carters and policemen. Lighter wear was manufactured for children. In 1899, about forty-five 'clickers' came out on strike because one of them had been discharged for declining to carry out the 'pricking' of footwear fronts. They claimed that the work was not included in an existing agreement and that there should be a premium payment. Following representations to two directors, the strike was soon settled. In 1910, the mills employed approximately 400 people.

Phelon & Moore Ltd, Horncastle Street, Cleckheaton. Local man John Carver Phelon, having unsuccessfully tried his hand at building a motorcar, switched to motorcycles. A keen cyclist, he had the idea of fitting a motor to a bicycle. Phelon teamed up with engineer Richard Moore and founded the firm Phelon & Moore, which went on to produce Panther motorcycles. In the above picture, from about 1915, women workers are assembling cycle wheels at the factory.

Phelon & Moore, Cleckheaton. During the First World War, the P&M works were entirely engaged in making motorcycles for HM Government. Above are a batch of near-completed machines and sidecars awaiting despatch to Brooklands for testing, before being handed over to the military authorities.

Eight

Transport

Liversedge Signal Box, *c.* 1908. Mainly built in timber, it is seen at the foot of a cutting, just south of Liversedge LNWR Station. Three signalmen, working shifts, staffed the cabin, and when time permited, they doubled as porters.

Heckmondwike Station, L&YR. The Lancashire & Yorkshire Railway was the first of two companies to construct a line through the Spen Valley. Opening in 1848, it ran from the Manchester & Leeds Railway at Mirfield to Low Moor, and then to Bradford. Three of its stations were in the Spen Valley – Heckmondwike, Liversedge and Cleckheaton. In the 1880s, Heckmondwike and Cleckheaton stations were completely rebuilt. Substantial alterations were made to Liversedge station in the 1890s. The above photograph of Heckmondwike station dates from around 1887. It shows a Tudor-style Victorian station with low platforms and interesting wall posters. When the new station opened in 1888, the old station became goods offices. As well as passengers, the L&YR provided facilities for handling raw materials and finished products for the valley's textile and other industries. None of this infrastructure deterred other railway companies from wanting a share of the business. The London & North Western Railway opened a branch along the Spen Valley in 1900, and provided additional stations at Heckmondwike, Liversedge and Cleckheaton, plus one at Gomersal, which previously had not been served by rail. Known officially as the Heaton Lodge & Wortley Railway (because it joined other lines at those points), it was dubbed the Leeds New Line, a name which stuck for many years. Heavily engineered, it ran along the opposite eastern side of the River Spen to the L&YR. The former LNWR lines in the Spen Valley were closed to passengers in 1953; those of the L&YR in 1965. Some freight facilities continued for a few more years. Road competition and a decline in local industries hastened the demise.

Heckmondwike Station, LNWR, *c.* 1905, looking towards the tunnel under High Street. Sited a short distance from the Market Place, the timber station buildings provided the usual facilities, such as stationmaster's office, ladies' and gents' waiting rooms, toilets and fire buckets (at left and right). The goods station, with cattle pens, loading stages and a cotton/wool warehouse, was 900yds away and reached from Walkley Lane.

The viaduct at Heckmondwike with the River Spen below, *c.* 1908. Carrying the London & North Western Railway, it was constructed just south of the goods station and made of iron/steel on brick pillars.

Liversedge Station, L&YR, looking south, *c*. 1906. The 1848 station was rebuilt on the same site in the mid-1890s. The photograph shows part-glazed canopies abutting on to the local sandstone buildings. Beyond the signal cabin (with a wool, grain and general warehouse to its left) the lines start to fan out towards loading stages.

Dymonds Siding, Strawberry Bank Colliery, Liversedge, *c*. 1911. The L&YR Spen Valley branch is shown below the embankment, with Railway Street and Edward Street at the back. The triangular junction gave direct access to the colliery and coke ovens to the south of Liversedge station.

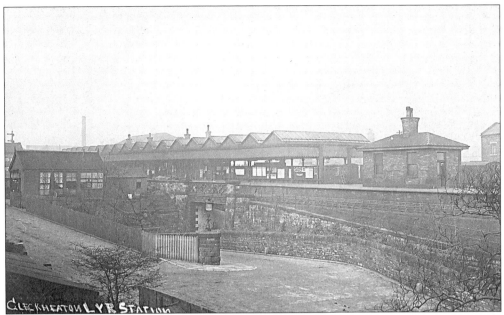

Cleckheaton Station, L&YR, *c.* 1904. Replacing the 1848 station, whose main building was similar to that at Heckmondwike (see page 104), the new station had an island platform, buildings down the centre and a ridge-and-furrow canopy with deep valances. The station is here seen from Tofts Road, with an underpass leading to Railway Street. Near the station were three warehouses, including one of three storeys and an outside hoist to lift goods from rail wagons.

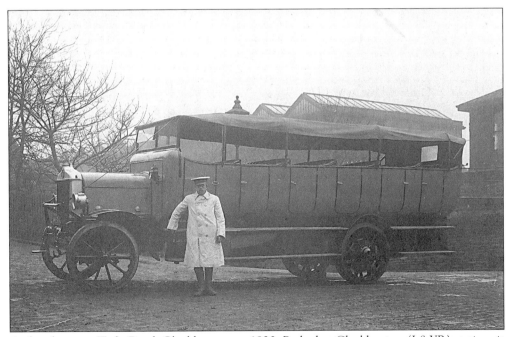

A charabanc on Tofts Road, Cleckheaton, *c.* 1920. Parked at Cleckheaton (L&YR) station, it has a solid-tyred AEC chassis and 12mph speed limit.

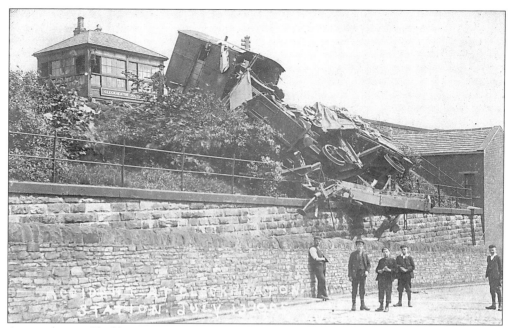

An accident at Cleckheaton Station, L&YR, 13 July 1905. During shunting operations, several loaded wagons ran out of control towards the bridge over Westgate and hit some buffers. Six trucks fell down the embankment overlooking Tofts Road, as shown. Nobody was hurt. The signal box in the background was erected in 1876.

The viaduct at Cleckheaton, c. 1910. To provide easier access to its station and goods yard, the LNWR constructed this viaduct to carry pedestrians and vehicles. It crossed a part of the Spen Valley known locally as the Bottoms.

Cleckheaton Station, LNWR, *c.* 1905. It is on the right, partly hidden by trees, with the line to the south running across the centre of the picture. Much of the town is shown at a lower level, with the Town Hall and Parish Church on the left. Contractors built a largely one-sided embankment, with a plateau, to take the railway.

Moorend from Cleckheaton (LNWR) Station, *c.* 1912. The station was situated to the left; the goods warehouse to the right. In between, and shown here, are various sections of track, loading banks and a cattle pen (painted white). In the distance, left, is Providence Place Congregational Chapel.

Bradford Road, Gomersal, looking south, *c.* 1910. Gomersal Station was adjacent to this railway bridge. Moor Lane, the approach to both platforms (connected by a subway) is off the picture to the right. After leaving the station, trains for Cleckheaton entered a tunnel which was 819yds long.

Gomersal Station, LNWR, *c.* 1903. As with other stations on the Leeds New Line, the construction of the building was mainly of timber which, when newly painted, produced an attractive effect. The station entrance is on the left. The goods yard and part of the warehouse are visible on the right. The yard was used by, among others, the local firm of Thomas Burnley.

Tramcar Depot, Frost Hill, Liversedge, 1903. Passenger-wise, the biggest threat to railways in the Spen Valley was electric trams. The Yorkshire (Woollen District) Electric Tramways Ltd was, by 1905, operating routes in the Cleckheaton, Heckmondwike, Liversedge, Gomersal and Birkenshaw areas. Large parts of the system were owned by various local councils. The tramcars belonged to the tramway company (with the exception of eight cars initially owned by Batley Corporation). The YWD was under some constraint from the British Electric Traction Co., of whom it was a subsidiary. The electric trams provided a useful service in the area for three decades. The newly-built depot for the Spen Valley trams is pictured above. To the left are the administrative buildings; on the right the actual sheds. Beyond the gateway, the single track fanned into ten sets of tracks, one set entering each of the ten bays, shown numbered 1 to 10 above the sliding doors. The featured tram, No. 37, is part of the company's first batch of double-deckers, Nos 7-48, delivered in 1902-03.

First tram through Cleckheaton, 7 April 1903. Tramcar No. 15, which probably had been running on the Thornhill (Dewsbury) route (note the indicator) attracts inquisitive sightseers as it climbs Bradford Road past the market. Old Bank Chambers, of Howarth & Howarth, architects, is on the left. The tramway through Cleckheaton officially opened on 24 April 1903.

The first tram to Gomersal, 2 October 1903. Excited children from the National School, left, line the footpath; pinafored ladies and cloth-capped men look on with fascination. This was a trial run, because the official opening date was a few weeks later.

Tramcar No. 42 of the YWD fleet at Littletown Post Office. It is in almost new condition, with curtains inside the windows and Leather's Patent Ventilators above them. Both these features were later removed. The batch of trams (Nos 7-48) was to a standard BET/Brush (of Loughborough) design, with longitudinal slatted seats downstairs and transverse wooden seats upstairs. The livery was crimson lake and cream.

Tramcar No. 19 at Birkenshaw terminus, Bradford Road, with driver Sam Cooper. The car, originally open-topped, has received a top cover, designed to fit inside the upper deck sides. The handbell near the driver replaces an earlier foot gong. These and other features suggest the photograph was taken at about the time of the First World War.

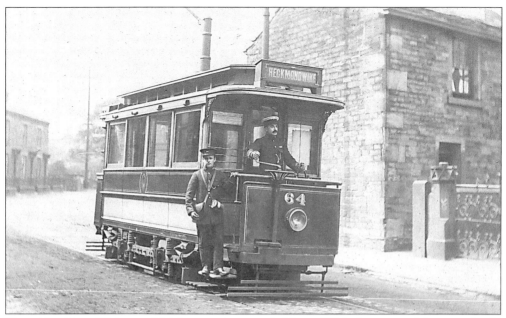

Tram No. 64 at Hightown Heights terminus, probably in 1905. An unusual feature, clearly visible, is the brake staff outside the dash. This tram, part of the Nos 60-65 batch, with special regenerative controls to reduce power consumption, was built in 1904 and seated twenty passengers.

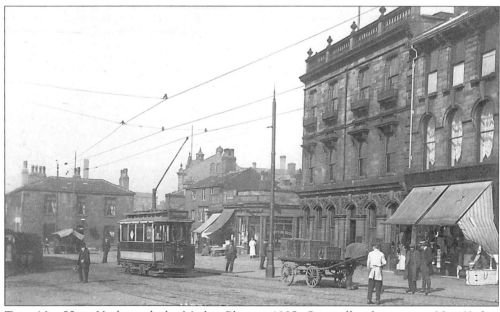

Tram No. 55 in Heckmondwike Market Place, c.1905. Originally, this car was No. 60, but swapped numbers with the first No. 55, which had suffered an accident. Here, the tramcar awaits departure for Hightown. The horse-drawn rulley is laden with baskets used in the textile trade.

Tramcar No. 46 at Moorend terminus, Bradford Road, Cleckheaton, *c*. 1928. The car is shown in its final form, with high upper-deck side and balcony panels, giving a relatively modern appearance. The livery had been changed to maroon and primrose.

Motorbus, Cleckheaton Market Place, *c*. 1914. Bearing fleet number 2, this formed part of the first batch of four buses purchased by Yorkshire Woollen District Transport Co. Ltd in 1913. The ramp helped elderly people to climb on to the high Daimler chassis.

Moorend, Cleckheaton, showing YWD motorbus No. 90 (HD 3428). This thirty-seater vehicle, on a Dennis chassis, was new in 1928, but gave only about six years service before being withdrawn. A 1938 YWD timetable states that accompanied drums, cellos, double basses, cricket bags and baskets of pigeons could be carried for 2d.

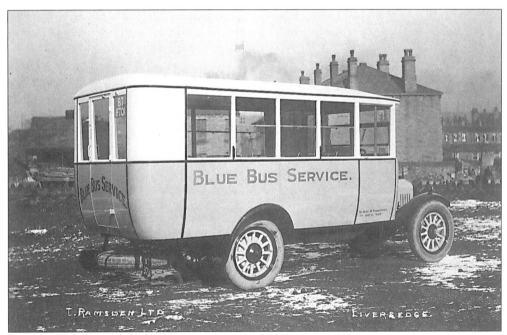

A motorbus built by J.Ramsden Ltd of Millbridge, a motor body building firm. The business was started by Joseph Ramsden, a wheelwright. The vehicle, seating eighteen passengers, was made around 1924 for Blue Bus Service of Bridlington and, before being driven there, it was photographed locally.

Nine
Events and People

Cleckheaton Victoria Prize Band in 1911. It developed from a band founded in 1849. Here, members proudly show off some of their trophies outside the Trades Hall, later called the Prospect Hall.

Golden Jubilee, Heckmondwike Co-operative Society, 13 August 1910. Well-groomed boys of the Millbridge division assemble in front of the Wesleyan Sunday School in Bennett Street, Millbridge, before participating in special celebrations in Heckmondwike. These included two processions, commencing at the Green, followed by entertainment in the cricket field.

Carnival float, c. 1907. The business of Sugden, Hepworth & Sugden, manufacturing confectioners of Cleckheaton, was founded around 1885 by two brothers and a brother-in-law. From the 1920s, the firm began to stock and distribute other leading makes of sweets and chocolate. A company cart is shown decorated for one of the Cleckheaton carnivals.

Charity carnival, Cleckheaton, 1908. Part of the procession is seen ascending Westgate, with Miss Harriet Exley's shop in the background. A small doll is suspended from the flag above the suffragette contraption.

Charity carnival, Cleckheaton, probably 1912. In the centre (with a man at the window) is Arthur Walker's butchering shop. On the left, a couple of Tom Hurley's removal vans form part of the parade. At extreme right, in front of the St John Ambulance Brigade, is the Cleckheaton ambulance.

Charabanc trip, 30 June 1912. Pub regulars await departure on the first charabanc trip from the Old Oak Inn at the end of Water Gate in Littletown (also see page 51).

Celebration, Oakenshaw. The cart carries the name of E.W. Lister & Co., who were worsted spinners at Oak Mills on Cliff Hollins Lane. It is shown decorated for a royal occasion, possibly the June 1911 Coronation.

Coronation bonfire, Scholes, Cleckheaton, Thursday 22 June 1911. Events were held throughout the Spen Valley to celebrate the accession to the throne of King George V and Queen Mary. This huge bonfire was erected on the recreation ground. Part of the 'chumping' was done by unemployed colliers. The pile was guarded night and day for a week to prevent premature ignition. It was lit shortly after 9pm by Miss Ethel Sharp, with a gold-tipped torch presented to her by George Whitely JP. A bullock was roasted (but not on the bonfire!) and 1,500 tickets were sold for beef sandwiches.

Royal visit to Heckmondwike. King George V and Queen Mary toured some industrial towns of the West Riding on 10 July 1912, arriving at Heckmondwike from Batley by late afternoon. A mounted policeman is featured clearing the way along Westgate, opposite the Green. Part of the Queen Hotel is visible on the left.

Royal visit to Heckmondwike, 10 July 1912. Crowds gather in Westgate, outside Althams store (at the corner with Regent Street). Althams, famous for their tea, were equally renowned for travelling requisites and railway tickets.

Royal visit to Littletown, 10 July 1912. Children from local schools sing the National Anthem on the broad area at the bottom of Listing Lane, in preparation for the passage of the royal pair along the main road in the foreground.

Royal visit to Cleckheaton, 10 July 1912. The families living in this small terrace on Northgate (also seen on page 15, top) combined to form this display. A few cherished aspidistras are visible.

Royal visit to Heckmondwike, 30 May 1918. Heckmondwike was on the itinerary of the royal couple's four-day wartime tour of West Riding industrial towns. Here, King George V and Queen Mary, having emerged from the first car, are welcomed on a carpeted platform in the Market Place.

Avro Biplane, Barley Fields, Heckmondwike, 1 October 1913. The pilot, F.P. Raynham, was flying from Gainsborough to Moortown, Leeds, to take part in an air race. Mistaking Heckmondwike for the Leeds area, he landed prematurely. Policemen controlled the crowd which gathered, until the plane was able to leave after seven hours.

A flood in Littletown, 1 August 1912. Following heavy rain, the River Spen burst its banks in several places, one of the worst hit areas being the centre of Littletown. In this view, looking up Water Gate (aptly named!), local people watch and wait.

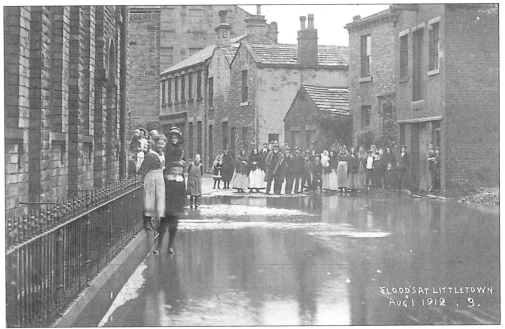

Another image of the flood in Littletown, 1 August 1912. A solitary sweeping brush is no match for the water in Carr Street. The United Methodist Sunday School, built in 1876, is on the left; this was demolished in 1971.

WHITE LEA LYDDITE EXPLOSION HECKMONDWIKE DEC^R 2ND 1914

AT MESSRS. HY. ELLISON L^{TD}

10 KILLED 6 INJURED.

ARTHUR COOPER, Builder

NIMROD FIRTH, Builder

JAMES NICHOLAS, Foreman

JOHN ED. MORTON

PERCY ASHTON   GEORGE TERRY   ALBERT FIRTH, Builder

About 2 o'clock to-day this terrible explosion occurred; so TERRIFIC was the FORCE that two men working on the roof of a house half-a-mile away were blown off, also WRECKING PROPERTY and SMASHING WINDOWS for MILES AROUND. The Firm were busy making Lyddite for the Government. The cause of the explosion has so far not yet been ascertained, but the buildings of the GRINDING ROOM and MAGAZINE were entirely DESTROYED, and some of the VICTIMS WERE BLOWN TO PIECES.

FRED WRIGHT, B.Sc., A.T.C., Chemist   WM. BERRY   CLIFFORD THOR...

The explosion which rocked White Lea, Heckmondwike, on 2 December 1914. White Lea Chemical Works, between Leeds Road and Leeds Old Road, were used by Henry Ellison Ltd during the Boer War (1899-1902) to manufacture picric acid for explosives. The works then lay largely unused until the outbreak of the First World War, when, at the government's request, Henry Ellison Ltd reopened them to make Lyddite from picric acid. On 2 December 1914, a terrific explosion devastated the works. Several buildings at the factory were destroyed completely, including the grinding room and magazine. Shock waves were felt for many miles around. The village of White Lea, 200yds away and separated from the works by fields, suffered severe damage. Ten men were killed, including some who were working on a house roof half a mile away. A further six men were badly injured. The official enquiry attributed the root of the blast to a piece of grit which caused a spark in a grinding machine. The Barnsley firm of Warner Gothard quickly produced the above postcard, which carries pictures of nine of the ten men who died. A batch of the cards was used to raise funds for destitute families.

The 1914 explosion at White Lea. With a sergeant and constable on guard, some of the old stone cottages damaged in the blast are shown. Windows and doors have virtually disintegrated.

White Lea after the explosion in 1914. This room, in one of the wrecked cottages, seems to have served as living quarters and bedroom. Part of a kitchen range is visible on the right.

This handsome Car, costing £600, Subscribed for by people of Spenborough, was presented by J. H. Collier, Esq., J.P. to Corps. Supt. E. Charlesworth for the St. John Ambulance Association on June 19th, 1915, for Service at the Front under the direction of H. D. Leather, Esq.

The Spenborough ambulance which cost £600, money which was subscribed by local people. It was displayed in Cleckheaton before being despatched to the French battlefields in 1915. Unfortunately, it became a 'casualty' of war and never returned.

The ambulance brigade, Cleckheaton. The photograph, which includes St John Ambulance members, was probably taken just before or during the First World War.